This Journal Belongs To:

Gratitude Journal

Journey 2 Free Publishing

ISBN - 978-1-954-553-16-3

Hi Young Queen,

My name is Larissa, and I wrote this journal for you. Having a positive attitude and the right mindset can change your life in a significant way. You are responsible for your thoughts, and your thoughts influence your actions. This is why it is really important that you develop the right mindset. Being in touch with your emotions, allowing yourself to feel those emotions, having self-control, and choosing to fill your mind with positive thoughts makes you a mentally strong individual. Your mind is the most powerful weapon you possess, and when you supercharge your mind with positivity, you become unstoppable. The prompts in this journal help you to develop a positive mindset, discover who you are, and encourage you to be kind, respectful, and grateful for the people and things in your life, no matter how great or small. Believe in yourself and your abilities. Know that there is greatness within you. I believe that you are capable and strong. You possess the ability to develop into a mindful, well-rounded, confident queen that will lead a happy, grounded, and fulfilled life. I love and appreciate you, young queen. Happy Journaling!

From my heart to yours - Larissa.

Children's Affirmation - I AM

You may use this affirmation page as a guide to fill in your daily affirmations.

Brave	Potentiality
Amazing	Strong
Awesome	Phenominal
Thoughtful	Special
Capable	Blessed
Dedicated	Unique
Confident	Resourceful
Treasured	Important
Brilliant	Bold
Intelligent	Loved
Determined	Mindful
Special	Creative
Enough	Forgiving
Honest	Talented
Kind	Follow My Heart
Encouraging	Helpful
Worthy	Kind To Myself
Original	Hardworking
Beautiful	Friendly
A Promise	Grateful
Compassionate	Ambitious
Resourceful	Admired
Resilient	Cherished
A Possibility	Appreciated
Smart	Respected

Date: ○ ○ ○ ○ ○ ○ ○
MON TUE WED THU FRI SAT SUN

Time: ⬭

Today I am Grateful for:

Today's Affirmation

My Happiness Scale:

☹ ☆ ☆ ☆ ☆ ☆ ☺

Best Moment Of the Day:

_____
_____
_____

Worst Moment Of the Day:

_____
_____
_____

This person brought me joy today:

_____
_____
_____

This happened today - Draw or write

My Happiness Scale:

☹ ☆ ☆ ☆ ☆ ☆ ☺

Date: ○ ○ ○ ○ ○ ○ ○
MON TUE WED THU FRI SAT SUN

Time:

Today I am Grateful for:

Today's Affirmation

My Happiness Scale:

☹ ☆ ☆ ☆ ☆ ☆ ☺

Best Moment Of the Day:

_____
_____
_____

Worst Moment Of the Day:

_____
_____
_____

This person brought me joy today:

_____
_____
_____

This happened today - Draw or write

_____
_____
_____
_____
_____
_____
_____
_____
_____
_____
_____
_____

My Happiness Scale:

☹ ☆ ☆ ☆ ☆ ☆ ☺

Date: ○ ○ ○ ○ ○ ○ ○
MON TUE WED THU FRI SAT SUN

Time:

Today I am Grateful for:

Today's Affirmation

My Happiness Scale:

☹ ☆ ☆ ☆ ☆ ☆ ☺

Best Moment Of the Day:

_____
_____
_____

Worst Moment Of the Day:

_____
_____
_____

This person brought me joy today:

_____
_____
_____

This happened today - Draw or write

_____
_____
_____
_____
_____
_____
_____
_____
_____
_____
_____
_____
_____

My Happiness Scale:

☹ ☆ ☆ ☆ ☆ ☆ ☺

Acknowledging the good that you already have in your life is the foundation for all abundance.

Eckhart Tolle

Date: ◯ ◯ ◯ ◯ ◯ ◯ ◯ **Time:** ⬭
MON TUE WED THU FRI SAT SUN

My Happiness Scale:

☹ ☆ ☆ ☆ ☆ ☆ ☺

I am Grateful for:

☐ Someone I love _ _ _ _ _ _ _ _ _ _ _ _ _

☐ Someone who helped me _ _ _ _ _ _ _ _ _ _ _ _

☐ A friend _ _ _ _ _ _ _ _ _ _ _ _

☐ Something I love to do _ _ _ _ _ _ _ _ _ _ _ _

☐ Something/someone that made me laugh _ _ _ _ _ _ _ _ _ _ _ _ _

☐ Something I like to eat, smell, touch, see and hear _ _ _ _ _ _ _

☐ Something warm and fuzzy _ _ _ _ _ _ _ _ _ _ _ _

Today, I chose to show love this way:

☐ I treated others with respect.　　☐ I showed love.

☐ I helped someone.　　☐ I used kind words.

☐ I was kind to someone.　　☐ I forgave someone.

☐ I apologized to someone.　　☐ I was appreciative.

I AM: ....

Date: ○ ○ ○ ○ ○ ○ ○
MON TUE WED THU FRI SAT SUN

Time: ⬭

Today I am Grateful for:

_____

_____

_____

_____

_____

Today's Affirmation

- -

- -

- -

- -

My Happiness Scale:

☹ ☆ ☆ ☆ ☆ ☆ ☺

Best Moment Of the Day:
_____
_____
_____

Worst Moment Of the Day:
_____
_____
_____

This person brought me joy today:
_____
_____
_____

This happened today - Draw or write

_____
_____
_____
_____
_____
_____
_____
_____
_____
_____
_____

My Happiness Scale:

☹ ☆ ☆ ☆ ☆ ☆ ☺

Date: ○ MON ○ TUE ○ WED ○ THU ○ FRI ○ SAT ○ SUN

Time: ⬭

~~~~~~

Today I am Grateful for:

~~~~~~

★ ## Today's Affirmation ★

My Happiness Scale:

☹ ☆ ☆ ☆ ☆ ☆ ☺

Best Moment Of the Day:

_____
_____
_____

Worst Moment Of the Day:

_____
_____
_____

This person brought me joy today:

_____
_____
_____

This happened today - Draw or write

_____
_____
_____
_____
_____
_____
_____
_____
_____
_____
_____
_____

My Happiness Scale:

☹ ☆ ☆ ☆ ☆ ☆ ☺

Date: ☐ MON ☐ TUE ☐ WED ☐ THU ☐ FRI ☐ SAT ☐ SUN   **Time:** ⬭

Today I am Grateful for:

....

....

....

....

....

Today's Affirmation

My Happiness Scale:

☹ ☆ ☆ ☆ ☆ ☆ ☺

Best Moment Of the Day:

_____
_____
_____
_____

Worst Moment Of the Day:

_____
_____
_____
_____

This person brought me joy today:

_____
_____
_____

This happened today - Draw or write

_____
_____
_____
_____
_____
_____
_____
_____
_____
_____
_____

My Happiness Scale:

☹ ☆ ☆ ☆ ☆ ☆ ☺

*Always remember that you are braver
than you believe, stronger than you
seem smarter than you think and loved
more than you know.*

 Christopher Robin

Date: ○ ○ ○ ○ ○ ○ ○
MON TUE WED THU FRI SAT SUN

Time: ⊂───⊃

My Happiness Scale:

☹ ☆ ☆ ☆ ☆ ☆ ☺

I am Grateful for:

□ Someone I love_____

□ Someone who helped me_____

□ A friend_____

□ Something I love to do_____

□ Something/someone that made me laugh_____

□ Something I like to eat, smell, touch, see and hear_____

□ Something warm and fuzzy_____

Today, I chose to show love this way:

□ I treated others with respect.   □ I showed love.

□ I helped someone.   □ I used kind words.

□ I was kind to someone.   □ I forgave someone.

□ I apologized to someone.   □ I was appreciative.

I AM:...

Date: ○ MON ○ TUE ○ WED ○ THU ○ FRI ○ SAT ○ SUN   **Time:** ⬭

Today I am Grateful for:

Today's Affirmation

My Happiness Scale:

☹ ☆ ☆ ☆ ☆ ☆ ☺

Best Moment Of the Day:

_____

_____

_____

Worst Moment Of the Day:

_____

_____

_____

This person brought me joy today:

_____

_____

_____

This happened today - Draw or write

My Happiness Scale:

☹ ☆ ☆ ☆ ☆ ☆ ☺

Date: ○ MON ○ TUE ○ WED ○ THU ○ FRI ○ SAT ○ SUN   **Time:**

Today I am Grateful for:

Today's Affirmation

My Happiness Scale:

☹ ☆ ☆ ☆ ☆ ☆ ☺

Best Moment Of the Day:

_____

_____

_____

Worst Moment Of the Day:

_____

_____

_____

This person brought me joy today:

_____

_____

This happened today - Draw or write

_____

_____

_____

_____

_____

_____

_____

_____

_____

_____

_____

_____

My Happiness Scale:

☹ ☆ ☆ ☆ ☆ ☆ ☺

Date: ○ MON ○ TUE ○ WED ○ THU ○ FRI ○ SAT ○ SUN   **Time:**

Today I am Grateful for:

....

....

....

....

....

Today's Affirmation

My Happiness Scale:

☹ ☆ ☆ ☆ ☆ ☆ ☺

Best Moment Of the Day:

_____
_____
_____

Worst Moment Of the Day:

_____
_____
_____

This person brought me joy today:

_____
_____
_____

This happened today - Draw or write

_____
_____
_____
_____
_____
_____
_____
_____
_____
_____
_____

My Happiness Scale:

☹ ☆ ☆ ☆ ☆ ☆ ☺

Confidence is the need to feel beautiful without someone needing to tell you.

Noor Bhambri

Date: ◯ ◯ ◯ ◯ ◯ ◯ ◯
MON TUE WED THU FRI SAT SUN

Time: ⬭

My Happiness Scale:

☹ ☆ ☆ ☆ ☆ ☆ ☺

I am Grateful for:

☐ Someone I love_____

☐ Someone who helped me_____

☐ A friend_____

☐ Something I love to do_____

☐ Something/someone that made me laugh_____

☐ Something I like to eat, smell, touch, see and hear_____

☐ Something warm and fuzzy_____

Today, I chose to show love this way:

☐ I treated others with respect.   ☐ I showed love.

☐ I helped someone.   ☐ I used kind words.

☐ I was kind to someone.   ☐ I forgave someone.

☐ I apologized to someone.   ☐ I was appreciative.

I AM:...

Date: ○ ○ ○ ○ ○ ○ ○
MON TUE WED THU FRI SAT SUN

Time:

Today I am Grateful for:

Today's Affirmation

My Happiness Scale:

☹ ☆ ☆ ☆ ☆ ☆ ☺

Best Moment Of the Day:

_____
_____
_____

Worst Moment Of the Day:

_____
_____
_____

This person brought me joy today:

_____
_____
_____

This happened today - Draw or write

_____
_____
_____
_____
_____
_____
_____
_____
_____
_____
_____
_____

My Happiness Scale:

☹ ☆ ☆ ☆ ☆ ☆ ☺

Date: ○ ○ ○ ○ ○ ○ ○
MON TUE WED THU FRI SAT SUN

Time: ⬭

Today I am Grateful for:

Today's Affirmation

My Happiness Scale:

☹ ☆ ☆ ☆ ☆ ☆ ☺

Best Moment Of the Day:

_____
_____
_____

Worst Moment Of the Day:

_____
_____
_____

This person brought me joy today:

_____
_____

This happened today - Draw or write

_____
_____
_____
_____
_____
_____
_____
_____
_____
_____
_____
_____
_____

My Happiness Scale:

☹ ☆ ☆ ☆ ☆ ☆ ☺

Date: ○ ○ ○ ○ ○ ○ ○
MON TUE WED THU FRI SAT SUN

Time:

Today I am Grateful for:

Today's Affirmation

My Happiness Scale:

☹ ☆ ☆ ☆ ☆ ☆ ☺

Best Moment Of the Day:

_____
_____
_____

Worst Moment Of the Day:

_____
_____
_____

This person brought me joy today:

_____
_____

This happened today - Draw or write

_____
_____
_____
_____
_____
_____
_____
_____
_____
_____
_____
_____

My Happiness Scale:

☹ ☆ ☆ ☆ ☆ ☆ ☺

You are amazing just the way you are

Billy Joel

My Happiness Scale:

☹ ☆ ☆ ☆ ☆ ☆ ☺

I am Grateful for:

☐ Someone I love _ _ _ _ _ _ _ _ _ _ _ _

☐ Someone who helped me _ _ _ _ _ _ _ _ _ _ _ _ _

☐ A friend _ _ _ _ _ _ _ _ _ _ _ _

☐ Something I love to do _ _ _ _ _ _ _ _ _ _ _ _

☐ Something/someone that made me laugh _ _ _ _ _ _ _ _ _ _ _ _ _

☐ Something I like to eat, smell, touch, see and hear _ _ _ _ _ _ _ _

☐ Something warm and fuzzy _ _ _ _ _ _ _ _ _ _ _ _

Today, I chose to show love this way:

☐ I treated others with respect.   ☐ I showed love.

☐ I helped someone.   ☐ I used kind words.

☐ I was kind to someone.   ☐ I forgave someone.

☐ I apologized to someone.   ☐ I was appreciative.

I AM: . . . .

Date: ○ MON ○ TUE ○ WED ○ THU ○ FRI ○ SAT ○ SUN **Time:**

Today I am Grateful for:

Today's Affirmation

My Happiness Scale:

☹ ☆ ☆ ☆ ☆ ☆ ☺

Best Moment Of the Day:

_____
_____
_____
_____

Worst Moment Of the Day:

_____
_____
_____
_____

This person brought me joy today:

_____
_____
_____
_____

This happened today - Draw or write

_____
_____
_____
_____
_____
_____
_____
_____
_____
_____
_____

My Happiness Scale:

☹ ☆ ☆ ☆ ☆ ☆ ☺

Date: ○ MON ○ TUE ○ WED ○ THU ○ FRI ○ SAT ○ SUN   **Time:**

Today I am Grateful for:

Today's Affirmation

My Happiness Scale:

☹ ☆ ☆ ☆ ☆ ☆ ☺

Best Moment Of the Day:

_____
_____
_____

Worst Moment Of the Day:

_____
_____
_____

This person brought me joy today:

_____
_____
_____

This happened today - Draw or write

_____
_____
_____
_____
_____
_____
_____
_____
_____
_____
_____
_____
_____

My Happiness Scale:

☹ ☆ ☆ ☆ ☆ ☆ ☺

Date: ○ MON ○ TUE ○ WED ○ THU ○ FRI ○ SAT ○ SUN

Time:

Today I am Grateful for:

Today's Affirmation

My Happiness Scale:

☹ ☆ ☆ ☆ ☆ ☆ ☺

Best Moment Of the Day:

_____

_____

_____

Worst Moment Of the Day:

_____

_____

_____

This person brought me joy today:

_____

_____

This happened today - Draw or write

_____

_____

_____

_____

_____

_____

_____

_____

_____

_____

_____

_____

My Happiness Scale:

☹ ☆ ☆ ☆ ☆ ☆ ☺

*It's not what happens to you but how
you react that matters.*

Epictetus

Date: ○ ○ ○ ○ ○ ○ ○
MON TUE WED THU FRI SAT SUN

Time: ⊂▭⊃

My Happiness Scale:

☹ ☆ ☆ ☆ ☆ ☆ ☺

I am Grateful for:

☐ Someone I love_____

☐ Someone who helped me_____

☐ A friend_____

☐ Something I love to do_____

☐ Something/someone that made me laugh_____

☐ Something I like to eat, smell, touch, see and hear_____

☐ Something warm and fuzzy_____

Today, I chose to show love this way:

☐ I treated others with respect. ☐ I showed love.

☐ I helped someone. ☐ I used kind words.

☐ I was kind to someone. ☐ I forgave someone.

☐ I apologized to someone. ☐ I was appreciative.

I AM:..

Date: ○ ○ ○ ○ ○ ○ ○
MON TUE WED THU FRI SAT SUN

Time: ⬭

Today I am Grateful for:

Today's Affirmation

My Happiness Scale:

☹ ☆ ☆ ☆ ☆ ☆ ☺

Best Moment Of the Day:

_____
_____
_____
_____

Worst Moment Of the Day:

_____
_____
_____
_____

This person brought me joy today:

_____
_____
_____

This happened today - Draw or write

_____
_____
_____
_____
_____
_____
_____
_____
_____
_____
_____
_____
_____

My Happiness Scale:

☹ ☆ ☆ ☆ ☆ ☆ ☺

Date: ○ MON ○ TUE ○ WED ○ THU ○ FRI ○ SAT ○ SUN **Time:** ⬭

Today I am Grateful for:

Today's Affirmation

My Happiness Scale:

☹ ☆ ☆ ☆ ☆ ☆ ☺

Best Moment Of the Day:

_____
_____
_____

Worst Moment Of the Day:

_____
_____
_____

This person brought me joy today:

_____
_____
_____

This happened today - Draw or write

My Happiness Scale:

☹ ☆ ☆ ☆ ☆ ☆ ☺

Date: ○ MON ○ TUE ○ WED ○ THU ○ FRI ○ SAT ○ SUN   **Time:**

Today I am Grateful for:

- -
- -
- -
- -
- -

Today's Affirmation

- -
- -
- -
- -

My Happiness Scale:

☹ ☆ ☆ ☆ ☆ ☆ ☺

Best Moment Of the Day:

_____
_____
_____
_____

Worst Moment Of the Day:

_____
_____
_____
_____

This person brought me joy today:

_____
_____
_____

This happened today - Draw or write

_____
_____
_____
_____
_____
_____
_____
_____
_____
_____
_____

My Happiness Scale:

☹ ☆ ☆ ☆ ☆ ☆ ☺

Change the world by being yourself.

Yoko Ono

My Happiness Scale:

☹ ☆ ☆ ☆ ☆ ☆ ☺

I am Grateful for:

☐ Someone I love_ _ _ _ _ _ _ _ _ _ _ _

☐ Someone who helped me_ _ _ _ _ _ _ _ _ _ _ _ _

☐ A friend_ _ _ _ _ _ _ _ _ _ _ _

☐ Something I love to do_ _ _ _ _ _ _ _ _ _ _ _

☐ Something/someone that made me laugh_ _ _ _ _ _ _ _ _ _ _ _

☐ Something I like to eat, smell, touch, see and hear_ _ _ _ _ _ _

☐ Something warm and fuzzy_ _ _ _ _ _ _ _ _ _ _ _

Today, I chose to show love this way:

☐ I treated others with respect.   ☐ I showed love.

☐ I helped someone.   ☐ I used kind words.

☐ I was kind to someone.   ☐ I forgave someone.

☐ I apologized to someone.   ☐ I was appreciative.

I AM:...

Date: ○ MON ○ TUE ○ WED ○ THU ○ FRI ○ SAT ○ SUN **Time:**

Today I am Grateful for:

Today's Affirmation

My Happiness Scale:

☹ ☆ ☆ ☆ ☆ ☆ ☺

Best Moment Of the Day:

_____
_____
_____

Worst Moment Of the Day:

_____
_____
_____

This person brought me joy today:

_____
_____
_____

This happened today - Draw or write

_____
_____
_____
_____
_____
_____
_____
_____
_____
_____
_____
_____
_____
_____
_____

My Happiness Scale:

☹ ☆ ☆ ☆ ☆ ☆ ☺

Date: ○ MON ○ TUE ○ WED ○ THU ○ FRI ○ SAT ○ SUN   **Time:** ⬭

Today I am Grateful for:

Today's Affirmation

My Happiness Scale:

☹ ☆ ☆ ☆ ☆ ☆ ☺

Best Moment Of the Day:

_____
_____
_____

Worst Moment Of the Day:

_____
_____
_____

This person brought me joy today:

_____
_____
_____

This happened today - Draw or write

My Happiness Scale:

☹ ☆ ☆ ☆ ☆ ☆ ☺

Date: ○ ○ ○ ○ ○ ○ ○
MON TUE WED THU FRI SAT SUN

Time:

Today I am Grateful for:

Today's Affirmation

My Happiness Scale:

☹ ☆ ☆ ☆ ☆ ☆ ☺

Best Moment Of the Day:

_____

_____

_____

Worst Moment Of the Day:

_____

_____

_____

This person brought me joy today:

_____

_____

_____

This happened today - Draw or write

_____

_____

_____

_____

_____

_____

_____

_____

_____

_____

_____

_____

My Happiness Scale:

☹ ☆ ☆ ☆ ☆ ☆ ☺

Integrity is doing the right thing even when no one is looking.

C.S. Lewis

Date: ○ ○ ○ ○ ○ ○ ○
MON TUE WED THU FRI SAT SUN

Time: ⬭

My Happiness Scale:

☹ ☆ ☆ ☆ ☆ ☆ ☺

I am Grateful for:

☐ Someone I love_____

☐ Someone who helped me_____

☐ A friend_____

☐ Something I love to do_____

☐ Something/someone that made me laugh_____

☐ Something I like to eat, smell, touch, see and hear_____

☐ Something warm and fuzzy_____

Today, I chose to show love this way:

☐ I treated others with respect.　　☐ I showed love.

☐ I helped someone.　　☐ I used kind words.

☐ I was kind to someone.　　☐ I forgave someone.

☐ I apologized to someone.　　☐ I was appreciative.

I AM:...

Date: ○ MON ○ TUE ○ WED ○ THU ○ FRI ○ SAT ○ SUN **Time:**

Today I am Grateful for:

Today's Affirmation

My Happiness Scale:

☹ ☆ ☆ ☆ ☆ ☆ ☺

Best Moment Of the Day:

_____

_____

_____

Worst Moment Of the Day:

_____

_____

_____

This person brought me joy today:

_____

_____

_____

This happened today - Draw or write

_____

_____

_____

_____

_____

_____

_____

_____

_____

_____

_____

_____

_____

_____

My Happiness Scale:

☹ ☆ ☆ ☆ ☆ ☆ ☺

Date: ○ ○ ○ ○ ○ ○ ○
MON TUE WED THU FRI SAT SUN

Time:

Today I am Grateful for:

- -
- -
- -
- -

Today's Affirmation

- -
- -
- -
- -

My Happiness Scale:

☹ ☆ ☆ ☆ ☆ ☆ ☺

Best Moment Of the Day:

_____
_____
_____

Worst Moment Of the Day:

_____
_____
_____

This person brought me joy today:

_____
_____

This happened today – Draw or write

_____
_____
_____
_____
_____
_____
_____
_____
_____
_____
_____
_____
_____

My Happiness Scale:

☹ ☆ ☆ ☆ ☆ ☆ ☺

Date: ○ MON ○ TUE ○ WED ○ THU ○ FRI ○ SAT ○ SUN

Time: ⬭

Today I am Grateful for:

Today's Affirmation

My Happiness Scale:

☹ ☆ ☆ ☆ ☆ ☆ ☺

Best Moment Of the Day:

_____

_____

_____

Worst Moment Of the Day:

_____

_____

_____

This person brought me joy today:

_____

_____

This happened today – Draw or write

_____

_____

_____

_____

_____

_____

_____

_____

_____

_____

_____

_____

_____

My Happiness Scale:

☹ ☆ ☆ ☆ ☆ ☆ ☺

Make today so awesome that yesterday becomes jealous and tomorrow can't wait to begin.

Barry Popik

Date: ○ ○ ○ ○ ○ ○ ○
MON TUE WED THU FRI SAT SUN **Time:** ⬭

My Happiness Scale:

☹ ☆ ☆ ☆ ☆ ☆ ☺

I am Grateful for:

☐ Someone I love _ _ _ _ _ _ _ _ _ _ _ _ _ _

☐ Someone who helped me _ _ _ _ _ _ _ _ _ _ _ _ _ _

☐ A friend _ _ _ _ _ _ _ _ _ _ _ _ _ _

☐ Something I love to do _ _ _ _ _ _ _ _ _ _ _ _ _ _

☐ Something/someone that made me laugh _ _ _ _ _ _ _ _ _ _ _ _ _ _

☐ Something I like to eat, smell, touch, see and hear _ _ _ _ _ _ _ _

☐ Something warm and fuzzy _ _ _ _ _ _ _ _ _ _ _ _ _ _

Today, I chose to show love this way:

☐ I treated others with respect. ☐ I showed love.

☐ I helped someone. ☐ I used kind words.

☐ I was kind to someone. ☐ I forgave someone.

☐ I apologized to someone. ☐ I was appreciative.

I AM: . . . .

Date: ○ MON ○ TUE ○ WED ○ THU ○ FRI ○ SAT ○ SUN   **Time:**

Today I am Grateful for:

Today's Affirmation

My Happiness Scale:

☹ ☆ ☆ ☆ ☆ ☆ ☺

Best Moment Of the Day:

_____
_____
_____

Worst Moment Of the Day:

_____
_____
_____

This person brought me joy today:

_____
_____

This happened today - Draw or write

My Happiness Scale:

☹ ☆ ☆ ☆ ☆ ☆ ☺

Date: ○ MON ○ TUE ○ WED ○ THU ○ FRI ○ SAT ○ SUN **Time:** ⬭

Today I am Grateful for:

Today's Affirmation

My Happiness Scale:

☹ ☆ ☆ ☆ ☆ ☆ ☺

Best Moment Of the Day:

_____
_____
_____

Worst Moment Of the Day:

_____
_____
_____

This person brought me joy today:

_____
_____
_____

This happened today - Draw or write

My Happiness Scale:

☹ ☆ ☆ ☆ ☆ ☆ ☺

Date: ○ MON ○ TUE ○ WED ○ THU ○ FRI ○ SAT ○ SUN **Time:** ⬭

Today I am Grateful for:

⭐ ## Today's Affirmation ⭐

My Happiness Scale:

☹ ☆ ☆ ☆ ☆ ☆ ☺

Best Moment Of the Day:

_____
_____
_____

Worst Moment Of the Day:

_____
_____
_____

This person brought me joy today:

_____
_____
_____

This happened today – Draw or write

My Happiness Scale:

☹ ☆ ☆ ☆ ☆ ☆ ☺

It's cool to be kind.

Sophia Amuroso

My Happiness Scale:

☹ ☆ ☆ ☆ ☆ ☆ ☺

I am Grateful for:

☐ Someone I love_____

☐ Someone who helped me_____

☐ A friend_____

☐ Something I love to do_____

☐ Something/someone that made me laugh_____

☐ Something I like to eat, smell, touch, see and hear_____

☐ Something warm and fuzzy_____

Today, I chose to show love this way:

☐ I treated others with respect.   ☐ I showed love.

☐ I helped someone.   ☐ I used kind words.

☐ I was kind to someone.   ☐ I forgave someone.

☐ I apologized to someone.   ☐ I was appreciative.

I AM:...

Date: ○ MON ○ TUE ○ WED ○ THU ○ FRI ○ SAT ○ SUN   **Time:**

Today I am Grateful for:

- -
- -
- -
- -

Today's Affirmation

- -
- -
- -
- -

My Happiness Scale:

☹ ☆ ☆ ☆ ☆ ☆ ☺

Best Moment Of the Day:

_____

_____

_____

Worst Moment Of the Day:

_____

_____

_____

This person brought me joy today:

_____

_____

_____

This happened today - Draw or write

My Happiness Scale:

☹ ☆ ☆ ☆ ☆ ☆ ☺

Date: ○ MON ○ TUE ○ WED ○ THU ○ FRI ○ SAT ○ SUN   **Time:**

Today I am Grateful for:

Today's Affirmation

My Happiness Scale:

☹ ☆ ☆ ☆ ☆ ☆ ☺

Best Moment Of the Day:

_____

_____

_____

Worst Moment Of the Day:

_____

_____

_____

This person brought me joy today:

_____

_____

_____

This happened today - Draw or write

_____

_____

_____

_____

_____

_____

_____

_____

_____

_____

_____

_____

_____

_____

My Happiness Scale:

☹ ☆ ☆ ☆ ☆ ☆ ☺

Date: ○ MON ○ TUE ○ WED ○ THU ○ FRI ○ SAT ○ SUN   **Time:** ⬭

Today I am Grateful for:

Today's Affirmation

My Happiness Scale:

☹ ☆ ☆ ☆ ☆ ☆ ☺

Best Moment Of the Day:

_____
_____
_____

Worst Moment Of the Day:

_____
_____
_____

This person brought me joy today:

_____
_____

This happened today - Draw or write

_____
_____
_____
_____
_____
_____
_____
_____
_____
_____
_____

My Happiness Scale:

☹ ☆ ☆ ☆ ☆ ☆ ☺

YOU GOT THIS.

Unknown

Date: ○ ○ ○ ○ ○ ○ ○
MON TUE WED THU FRI SAT SUN

Time:

My Happiness Scale:

☹ ☆ ☆ ☆ ☆ ☆ ☺

I am Grateful for:

□ Someone I love_____

□ Someone who helped me_____

□ A friend_____

□ Something I love to do_____

□ Something/someone that made me laugh_____

□ Something I like to eat, smell, touch, see and hear_____

□ Something warm and fuzzy_____

Today, I chose to show love this way:

□ I treated others with respect.   □ I showed love.

□ I helped someone.   □ I used kind words.

□ I was kind to someone.   □ I forgave someone.

□ I apologized to someone.   □ I was appreciative.

I AM:..

Date: ○ MON ○ TUE ○ WED ○ THU ○ FRI ○ SAT ○ SUN **Time:**

Today I am Grateful for:

Today's Affirmation

My Happiness Scale:

☹ ☆ ☆ ☆ ☆ ☆ ☺

Best Moment Of the Day:

_____
_____
_____

Worst Moment Of the Day:

_____
_____
_____

This person brought me joy today:

_____
_____
_____

This happened today - Draw or write

_____
_____
_____
_____
_____
_____
_____
_____
_____
_____
_____
_____

My Happiness Scale:

☹ ☆ ☆ ☆ ☆ ☆ ☺

Date: ○ MON ○ TUE ○ WED ○ THU ○ FRI ○ SAT ○ SUN   **Time:** ⬭

Today I am Grateful for:

Today's Affirmation

My Happiness Scale:

☹ ☆ ☆ ☆ ☆ ☆ ☺

Best Moment Of the Day:

_____
_____
_____

Worst Moment Of the Day:

_____
_____
_____

This person brought me joy today:

_____
_____
_____

This happened today – Draw or write

My Happiness Scale:

☹ ☆ ☆ ☆ ☆ ☆ ☺

Date: ○ MON ○ TUE ○ WED ○ THU ○ FRI ○ SAT ○ SUN   **Time:** ⊂⊃

Today I am Grateful for:

Today's Affirmation

My Happiness Scale:

☹ ☆ ☆ ☆ ☆ ☆ ☺

Best Moment Of the Day:

_____
_____
_____
_____

Worst Moment Of the Day:

_____
_____
_____
_____

This person brought me joy today:

_____
_____
_____

This happened today - Draw or write

_____
_____
_____
_____
_____
_____
_____
_____
_____
_____
_____
_____

My Happiness Scale:

☹ ☆ ☆ ☆ ☆ ☆ ☺

Kindness is love in action.

Kim Balstad

Date: ◯ ◯ ◯ ◯ ◯ ◯ ◯
MON TUE WED THU FRI SAT SUN

Time: ⬭

My Happiness Scale:

☹ ☆ ☆ ☆ ☆ ☆ ☺

I am Grateful for:

□ Someone I love_____

□ Someone who helped me_____

□ A friend_____

□ Something I love to do_____

□ Something/someone that made me laugh_____

□ Something I like to eat, smell, touch, see and hear_____

□ Something warm and fuzzy_____

Today, I chose to show love this way:

□ I treated others with respect.   □ I showed love.

□ I helped someone.   □ I used kind words.

□ I was kind to someone.   □ I forgave someone.

□ I apologized to someone.   □ I was appreciative.

I AM:..

Date: ◯ ◯ ◯ ◯ ◯ ◯ ◯
MON TUE WED THU FRI SAT SUN   Time:

Today I am Grateful for:

Today's Affirmation

My Happiness Scale:

☹ ☆ ☆ ☆ ☆ ☆ ☺

Best Moment Of the Day:

_____
_____
_____

Worst Moment Of the Day:

_____
_____
_____

This person brought me joy today:

_____
_____

This happened today - Draw or write

_____
_____
_____
_____
_____
_____
_____
_____
_____
_____
_____
_____

My Happiness Scale:

☹ ☆ ☆ ☆ ☆ ☆ ☺

Date: ○ MON ○ TUE ○ WED ○ THU ○ FRI ○ SAT ○ SUN **Time:** ⬭

Today I am Grateful for:

Today's Affirmation

My Happiness Scale:

☹ ☆ ☆ ☆ ☆ ☆ ☺

Best Moment Of the Day:

_____
_____
_____

Worst Moment Of the Day:

_____
_____
_____

This person brought me joy today:

_____
_____

This happened today – Draw or write

My Happiness Scale:

☹ ☆ ☆ ☆ ☆ ☆ ☺

Date: ○ MON ○ TUE ○ WED ○ THU ○ FRI ○ SAT ○ SUN   **Time:** ▭

Today I am Grateful for:

- -

- -

- -

- -

- -

Today's Affirmation

- -

- -

- -

- -

My Happiness Scale:

☹ ☆ ☆ ☆ ☆ ☆ ☺

Best Moment Of the Day:

_____
_____
_____
_____

Worst Moment Of the Day:

_____
_____
_____
_____

This person brought me joy today:

_____
_____
_____

This happened today – Draw or write

_____
_____
_____
_____
_____
_____
_____
_____
_____
_____
_____
_____

My Happiness Scale:

☹ ☆ ☆ ☆ ☆ ☆ ☺

Don't dim your light because others think it's too bright.

Jackie Cantoni

Date: ○ ○ ○ ○ ○ ○ ○
MON TUE WED THU FRI SAT SUN

Time: ⬭

My Happiness Scale:

☹ ☆ ☆ ☆ ☆ ☆ ☺

I am Grateful for:

☐ Someone I love_ _ _ _ _ _ _ _ _ _ _ _ _

☐ Someone who helped me_ _ _ _ _ _ _ _ _ _ _ _ _ _

☐ A friend_ _ _ _ _ _ _ _ _ _ _ _ _

☐ Something I love to do_ _ _ _ _ _ _ _ _ _ _ _ _

☐ Something/someone that made me laugh_ _ _ _ _ _ _ _ _ _ _ _ _

☐ Something I like to eat, smell, touch, see and hear_ _ _ _ _ _ _

☐ Something warm and fuzzy_ _ _ _ _ _ _ _ _ _ _ _ _

Today, I chose to show love this way:

☐ I treated others with respect.   ☐ I showed love.

☐ I helped someone.   ☐ I used kind words.

☐ I was kind to someone.   ☐ I forgave someone.

☐ I apologized to someone.   ☐ I was appreciative.

I AM:...

Date: ○ MON ○ TUE ○ WED ○ THU ○ FRI ○ SAT ○ SUN   **Time:** ⬭

Today I am Grateful for:

Today's Affirmation

My Happiness Scale:

☹ ☆ ☆ ☆ ☆ ☆ ☺

Best Moment Of the Day:

_____

_____

_____

Worst Moment Of the Day:

_____

_____

_____

This person brought me joy today:

_____

_____

_____

This happened today - Draw or write

_____

_____

_____

_____

_____

_____

_____

_____

_____

_____

_____

_____

My Happiness Scale:

☹ ☆ ☆ ☆ ☆ ☆ ☺

Date: ○ ○ ○ ○ ○ ○ ○
MON TUE WED THU FRI SAT SUN

Time:

Today I am Grateful for:

Today's Affirmation

My Happiness Scale:

☹ ☆ ☆ ☆ ☆ ☆ ☺

Best Moment Of the Day:

_____
_____
_____
_____

Worst Moment Of the Day:

_____
_____
_____
_____

This person brought me joy today:

_____
_____
_____

This happened today – Draw or write

_____
_____
_____
_____
_____
_____
_____
_____
_____
_____
_____

My Happiness Scale:

☹ ☆ ☆ ☆ ☆ ☆ ☺

Date: ○ MON ○ TUE ○ WED ○ THU ○ FRI ○ SAT ○ SUN **Time:**

Today I am Grateful for:

Today's Affirmation

My Happiness Scale:

☹ ☆ ☆ ☆ ☆ ☆ ☺

Best Moment Of the Day:

_____
_____
_____

Worst Moment Of the Day:

_____
_____
_____

This person brought me joy today:

_____
_____

This happened today - Draw or write

_____
_____
_____
_____
_____
_____
_____
_____
_____
_____

My Happiness Scale:

☹ ☆ ☆ ☆ ☆ ☆ ☺

*Don't let what you can't do stop you
from doing what you can do.*

John Wooden

Date: ○ ○ ○ ○ ○ ○ ○
MON TUE WED THU FRI SAT SUN

Time: ⟨___⟩

My Happiness Scale:

☹ ☆ ☆ ☆ ☆ ☆ ☺

I am Grateful for:

☐ Someone I love_____

☐ Someone who helped me_____

☐ A friend_____

☐ Something I love to do_____

☐ Something/someone that made me laugh_____

☐ Something I like to eat, smell, touch, see and hear_____

☐ Something warm and fuzzy_____

Today, I chose to show love this way:

☐ I treated others with respect.   ☐ I showed love.

☐ I helped someone.   ☐ I used kind words.

☐ I was kind to someone.   ☐ I forgave someone.

☐ I apologized to someone.   ☐ I was appreciative.

I AM:...

Date: ○ ○ ○ ○ ○ ○ ○
MON TUE WED THU FRI SAT SUN **Time:**

Today I am Grateful for:

Today's Affirmation

My Happiness Scale:

☹ ☆ ☆ ☆ ☆ ☆ ☺

Best Moment Of the Day:

_____
_____
_____

Worst Moment Of the Day:

_____
_____
_____

This person brought me joy today:

_____
_____
_____

This happened today - Draw or write

_____
_____
_____
_____
_____
_____
_____
_____
_____
_____
_____

My Happiness Scale:

☹ ☆ ☆ ☆ ☆ ☆ ☺

Date: ○ ○ ○ ○ ○ ○ ○ Time: ____
MON TUE WED THU FRI SAT SUN

Today I am Grateful for:

Today's Affirmation

My Happiness Scale:

☹ ☆ ☆ ☆ ☆ ☆ ☺

Best Moment Of the Day:

_____
_____
_____

Worst Moment Of the Day:

_____
_____
_____

This person brought me joy today:

_____
_____
_____

This happened today - Draw or write

My Happiness Scale:

☹ ☆ ☆ ☆ ☆ ☆ ☺

Date: ○ MON ○ TUE ○ WED ○ THU ○ FRI ○ SAT ○ SUN   **Time:** ⬭

Today I am Grateful for:

Today's Affirmation

My Happiness Scale:

☹ ☆ ☆ ☆ ☆ ☆ ☺

Best Moment Of the Day:

_____

_____

_____

Worst Moment Of the Day:

_____

_____

_____

This person brought me joy today:

_____

_____

_____

This happened today - Draw or write

My Happiness Scale:

☹️ ☆ ☆ ☆ ☆ ☆ 🙂

Do what you can, with what you have, where you are.

Theodore Roosevelt

My Happiness Scale:

☹ ☆ ☆ ☆ ☆ ☆ ☺

I am Grateful for:

☐ Someone I love_____

☐ Someone who helped me_____

☐ A friend_____

☐ Something I love to do_____

☐ Something/someone that made me laugh_____

☐ Something I like to eat, smell, touch, see and hear_____

☐ Something warm and fuzzy_____

Today, I chose to show love this way:

☐ I treated others with respect.   ☐ I showed love.

☐ I helped someone.   ☐ I used kind words.

☐ I was kind to someone.   ☐ I forgave someone.

☐ I apologized to someone.   ☐ I was appreciative.

I AM:..

Date: ○ MON ○ TUE ○ WED ○ THU ○ FRI ○ SAT ○ SUN   **Time:** ⬭

Today I am Grateful for:

Today's Affirmation

My Happiness Scale:

☹ ☆ ☆ ☆ ☆ ☆ ☺

Best Moment Of the Day:

_____
_____
_____

Worst Moment Of the Day:

_____
_____
_____

This person brought me joy today:

_____
_____

This happened today – Draw or write

_____
_____
_____
_____
_____
_____
_____
_____
_____
_____
_____
_____
_____

My Happiness Scale:

☹ ☆ ☆ ☆ ☆ ☆ ☺

Date: ○ ○ ○ ○ ○ ○ ○
MON TUE WED THU FRI SAT SUN

Time:

Today I am Grateful for:

Today's Affirmation

My Happiness Scale:

☹ ☆ ☆ ☆ ☆ ☆ ☺

Best Moment Of the Day:

_____
_____
_____

Worst Moment Of the Day:

_____
_____
_____

This person brought me joy today:

_____
_____

This happened today - Draw or write

_____
_____
_____
_____
_____
_____
_____
_____
_____
_____
_____
_____
_____

My Happiness Scale:

☹ ☆ ☆ ☆ ☆ ☆ ☺

Today I am Grateful for:

Today's Affirmation

My Happiness Scale:

☹ ☆ ☆ ☆ ☆ ☆ ☺

Best Moment Of the Day:

_____

_____

_____

Worst Moment Of the Day:

_____

_____

_____

This person brought me joy today:

_____

_____

_____

This happened today - Draw or write

_____

_____

_____

_____

_____

_____

_____

_____

_____

_____

_____

My Happiness Scale:

☹ ☆ ☆ ☆ ☆ ☆ ☺

You always pass failure on the way to success.

Mickey Rooney

Date: ○ ○ ○ ○ ○ ○ ○
MON TUE WED THU FRI SAT SUN

Time: ⬭

My Happiness Scale:

☹ ☆ ☆ ☆ ☆ ☆ ☺

I am Grateful for:

☐ Someone I love_ _ _ _ _ _ _ _ _ _ _ _ _

☐ Someone who helped me_ _ _ _ _ _ _ _ _ _ _ _ _

☐ A friend_ _ _ _ _ _ _ _ _ _ _ _ _

☐ Something I love to do_ _ _ _ _ _ _ _ _ _ _ _ _

☐ Something/someone that made me laugh_ _ _ _ _ _ _ _ _ _ _ _ _

☐ Something I like to eat, smell, touch, see and hear_ _ _ _ _ _ _

☐ Something warm and fuzzy_ _ _ _ _ _ _ _ _ _ _ _ _

Today, I chose to show love this way:

☐ I treated others with respect.　　☐ I showed love.

☐ I helped someone.　　☐ I used kind words.

☐ I was kind to someone.　　☐ I forgave someone.

☐ I apologized to someone.　　☐ I was appreciative.

I AM:...

Date: ○ ○ ○ ○ ○ ○ ○
MON TUE WED THU FRI SAT SUN

Time: ⬭

Today I am Grateful for:

Today's Affirmation

My Happiness Scale:

☹ ☆ ☆ ☆ ☆ ☆ ☺

Best Moment Of the Day:

_____
_____
_____

Worst Moment Of the Day:

_____
_____
_____

This person brought me joy today:

_____
_____
_____

This happened today - Draw or write

_____
_____
_____
_____
_____
_____
_____
_____
_____
_____
_____
_____

My Happiness Scale:

☹ ☆ ☆ ☆ ☆ ☆ ☺

Date: ○ MON ○ TUE ○ WED ○ THU ○ FRI ○ SAT ○ SUN   **Time:** ▭

Today I am Grateful for:

Today's Affirmation

My Happiness Scale:

☹ ☆ ☆ ☆ ☆ ☆ ☺

Best Moment Of the Day:

_____
_____
_____

Worst Moment Of the Day:

_____
_____
_____

This person brought me joy today:

_____
_____
_____

This happened today - Draw or write

_____
_____
_____
_____
_____
_____
_____
_____
_____
_____
_____
_____
_____

My Happiness Scale:

☹ ☆ ☆ ☆ ☆ ☺

Date: ○ MON ○ TUE ○ WED ○ THU ○ FRI ○ SAT ○ SUN   **Time:**

Today I am Grateful for:

Today's Affirmation

My Happiness Scale:

☹ ☆ ☆ ☆ ☆ ☆ ☺

Best Moment Of the Day:

_____
_____
_____

Worst Moment Of the Day:

_____
_____
_____

This person brought me joy today:

_____
_____
_____

This happened today - Draw or write

_____
_____
_____
_____
_____
_____
_____
_____
_____
_____
_____
_____
_____

My Happiness Scale:

☹ ☆ ☆ ☆ ☆ ☆ ☺

Make each day your masterpiece.

John Wooden

My Happiness Scale:

☹ ☆ ☆ ☆ ☆ ☆ ☺

I am Grateful for:

□ Someone I love_____

□ Someone who helped me_____

□ A friend_____

□ Something I love to do_____

□ Something/someone that made me laugh_____

□ Something I like to eat, smell, touch, see and hear_____

□ Something warm and fuzzy_____

Today, I chose to show love this way:

□ I treated others with respect.   □ I showed love.

□ I helped someone.   □ I used kind words.

□ I was kind to someone.   □ I forgave someone.

□ I apologized to someone.   □ I was appreciative.

I AM:..

Date: ○ ○ ○ ○ ○ ○ ○
MON TUE WED THU FRI SAT SUN

Time: ⬭

Today I am Grateful for:

Today's Affirmation

My Happiness Scale:

☹ ☆ ☆ ☆ ☆ ☆ ☺

Best Moment Of the Day:

_____
_____
_____

Worst Moment Of the Day:

_____
_____
_____

This person brought me joy today:

_____
_____
_____

This happened today - Draw or write

_____
_____
_____
_____
_____
_____
_____
_____
_____
_____
_____
_____
_____
_____

My Happiness Scale:

☹ ☆ ☆ ☆ ☆ ☆ ☺

Date: ○ ○ ○ ○ ○ ○ ○
MON TUE WED THU FRI SAT SUN

Time:

Today I am Grateful for:

Today's Affirmation

My Happiness Scale:

☹ ☆ ☆ ☆ ☆ ☆ ☺

Best Moment Of the Day:

_____
_____
_____

Worst Moment Of the Day:

_____
_____
_____

This person brought me joy today:

_____
_____
_____

This happened today – Draw or write

_____
_____
_____
_____
_____
_____
_____
_____
_____
_____
_____

My Happiness Scale:

☹ ☆ ☆ ☆ ☆ ☆ ☺

Date: ○ MON ○ TUE ○ WED ○ THU ○ FRI ○ SAT ○ SUN

Time:

Today I am Grateful for:

Today's Affirmation

My Happiness Scale:

☹ ☆ ☆ ☆ ☆ ☆ ☺

Best Moment Of the Day:

_____
_____
_____

Worst Moment Of the Day:

_____
_____
_____

This person brought me joy today:

_____
_____
_____

This happened today – Draw or write

_____
_____
_____
_____
_____
_____
_____
_____
_____
_____
_____
_____
_____

My Happiness Scale:

☹ ☆ ☆ ☆ ☆ ☆ ☺

No one is perfect – that's why pencils have erasers.

Wolfgang Riebe

Date: ☐ MON ☐ TUE ☐ WED ☐ THU ☐ FRI ☐ SAT ☐ SUN **Time:** ⬭

My Happiness Scale:

☹ ☆ ☆ ☆ ☆ ☆ ☺

I am Grateful for:

☐ Someone I love_____

☐ Someone who helped me_____

☐ A friend_____

☐ Something I love to do_____

☐ Something/someone that made me laugh_____

☐ Something I like to eat, smell, touch, see and hear_____

☐ Something warm and fuzzy_____

Today, I chose to show love this way:

☐ I treated others with respect.   ☐ I showed love.

☐ I helped someone.   ☐ I used kind words.

☐ I was kind to someone.   ☐ I forgave someone.

☐ I apologized to someone.   ☐ I was appreciative.

I AM:..

Date:

○ ○ ○ ○ ○ ○ ○
MON TUE WED THU FRI SAT SUN

Time:

Today I am Grateful for:

Today's Affirmation

My Happiness Scale:

☹ ☆ ☆ ☆ ☆ ☆ ☺

Best Moment Of the Day:

_____
_____
_____

Worst Moment Of the Day:

_____
_____
_____

This person brought me joy today:

_____
_____
_____

This happened today - Draw or write

_____
_____
_____
_____
_____
_____
_____
_____
_____
_____
_____
_____

My Happiness Scale:

☹ ☆ ☆ ☆ ☆ ☆ ☺

Date: ○ MON ○ TUE ○ WED ○ THU ○ FRI ○ SAT ○ SUN   **Time:** ⬭

Today I am Grateful for:

Today's Affirmation

My Happiness Scale:

☹ ☆ ☆ ☆ ☆ ☆ ☺

Best Moment Of the Day:

_____

_____

_____

Worst Moment Of the Day:

_____

_____

_____

This person brought me joy today:

_____

_____

_____

This happened today – Draw or write

_____

_____

_____

_____

_____

_____

_____

_____

_____

_____

_____

_____

_____

_____

My Happiness Scale:

☹ ☆ ☆ ☆ ☆ ☆ ☺

Date: ○ ○ ○ ○ ○ ○ ○
MON TUE WED THU FRI SAT SUN

Time:

Today I am Grateful for:

Today's Affirmation

My Happiness Scale:

☹ ☆ ☆ ☆ ☆ ☆ ☺

Best Moment Of the Day:

_____
_____
_____

Worst Moment Of the Day:

_____
_____
_____

This person brought me joy today:

_____
_____
_____

This happened today – Draw or write

_____
_____
_____
_____
_____
_____
_____
_____
_____
_____
_____
_____
_____
_____
_____
_____

My Happiness Scale:

☹ ☆ ☆ ☆ ☆ ☆ ☺

Acknowledging the good that you already have in your life is the foundation for all abundance.

Eckhart Tolle

Date: ○ ○ ○ ○ ○ ○ ○
MON TUE WED THU FRI SAT SUN

Time: ⬭

My Happiness Scale:

☹ ☆ ☆ ☆ ☆ ☆ ☺

I am Grateful for:

☐ Someone I love_ _ _ _ _ _ _ _ _ _ _ _ _

☐ Someone who helped me_ _ _ _ _ _ _ _ _ _ _ _ _

☐ A friend_ _ _ _ _ _ _ _ _ _ _ _ _

☐ Something I love to do_ _ _ _ _ _ _ _ _ _ _ _ _

☐ Something/someone that made me laugh_ _ _ _ _ _ _ _ _ _ _ _ _

☐ Something I like to eat, smell, touch, see and hear_ _ _ _ _ _ _

☐ Something warm and fuzzy_ _ _ _ _ _ _ _ _ _ _ _ _

Today, I chose to show love this way:

☐ I treated others with respect.   ☐ I showed love.

☐ I helped someone.   ☐ I used kind words.

☐ I was kind to someone.   ☐ I forgave someone.

☐ I apologized to someone.   ☐ I was appreciative.

I AM:...

Definitions:

grat·i·tude: is pausing to notice and appreciate the things that we often take for granted, like having a place to live, food, clean water, friends, family, even computer access.

mind·ful·ness: paying full attention to something. It means slowing down to really notice what you're doing. Being mindful is the opposite of rushing or multitasking.

thank·ful: feeling or showing thanks; grateful. We are thankful for our good health

re·spect: - is the ability to recognize and appreciate the rights, beliefs, practices, and differences of other people. Due regard for the feelings, wishes, rights, or traditions of others. These are important, but respect means more than just tolerating or accepting a person.

af·firm·a·tion: - noun: affirmation; plural noun: affirmations
1. the action or process of affirming something or someone or being affirmed. " I am strong' or "he nodded in affirmation"

THINGS I'M GOOD AT (MY STRENGTHS):
THINGS I NEED TO WORK ON - (MY WEAKNESSES):

Every human being is flawed. No one is perfect! Men, women and children - we all have things we do well and other things we are not so good at. We have strengths - the things we are great at and weaknesses - things that aren't as easy.

Circle your strengths and draw a line through you weaknesses

Helping others	Fixing things
Listening	Playing an instrument
Art	Dancing
Painting	Communicating my feelings
Creating Things	Using technology
Baking	Telling the truth
Doing my chores	Keeping my hands to myself
Thinking positively	Speaking up
Doing my homework	Using Self -Control
Making friends	Organization
Reading	Being on Time
Allowing others to speak	Making people laugh
Sharing	Eating healthy
Working with others	Feeling Confident
Standing up for myself	Resting and Relaxing
Sticking up for others	Speaking in public
Being patient	Never giving up
Being a leader	Thinking for myself
Playing sports	Eating healthy
Writing	Listening to others
Staying focused	Math
Easily distracted	Listening to my gut
Trying again	

Titles by the Same Author:

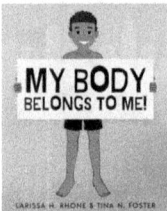

My Body Belongs To Me!
This book sensitively tackles the subject of safe and unsafe touch, body ownership, healthy boundaries, communication, private parts and assist parents, caregivers, and educators to broach this subject with children in a non-threatening and age-appropriate way. Discussion Questions included.
Ages 3-7 years

Children Have Rights Too!
A children's comic book that empowers and teaches children about respect, personal body safety, private parts, safe and unsafe touch, secrets, feelings, and using their voices to speak up if made to feel uncomfortable.
Discussion Questions and Activities included.
Ages 8 to 12 years old.

Unwind
Children Are Stressed Too! Help your little ones UNWIND with this children's mindfulness coloring book. Designs include Mandalas. Animals, Flowers, Nature, and Much More. It provides hours of fun, calm, anxiety-reducing, and relaxation through creative expression. Designs range in complexity and detail from beginner to advance level.
Ages 6-12 years old.

SELF-SOOTHE: Volume 1
There are many ways to Self-Soothe when triggered, feeling unhappy, anxious, or distressed. This adult coloring book from Journey 2 Free Publishing has 50 birds and butterflies designs to promote Self -Care. Soothe thyself within these pages. This book provides hours of fun, relaxation, and stress relief through creative expression. Give yourself permission to breathe, release and reset.
For - Adults and Teens

Self-Soothe Volume 2
There are many ways to Self-Soothe when triggered, feeling unhappy, anxious, or distressed. This adult coloring book from Journey 2 Free Publishing has 50 designs to promote Self -Care. Soothe thyself within these pages. This book provides hours of fun, relaxation, and stress relief through creative expression. Give yourself permission to breathe, release and reset.
For - Adults and Teens

For more information, visit: www.journey2free.com

Follow us on Instagram @journey2freepublishing & @brosjhaydnjo